If I Were a Polar Bear

By Meg Gaertner

level 2 little blue readers

www.littlebluehousebooks.com

Little Blue House is distributed by North Star Editions:
sales@northstareditions.com | 888-417-0195

Produced for Little Blue House by Red Line Editorial.

Photographs ©: Shutterstock Images, cover, 17 (top), 17 (bottom), 20–21, 24 (bottom right); iStockphoto, 4, 6–7, 9, 10 (top), 10 (bottom), 13, 14–15, 18 (top), 18 (bottom), 23, 24 (top left), 24 (top right), 24 (bottom left)

Library of Congress Control Number: 2020913852

ISBN
978-1-64619-305-9 (hardcover)
978-1-64619-323-3 (paperback)
978-1-64619-359-2 (ebook pdf)
978-1-64619-341-7 (hosted ebook)

Printed in the United States of America
Mankato, MN
012021

About the Author

Meg Gaertner enjoys reading, writing, dancing, and being outside. She thinks polar bears are very cute. She lives in Minnesota.

Table of Contents

If I Were a Polar Bear

I would live on ice

by the ocean.

I would walk on the ice, and I

would swim in the water.

I would have thick fur.

It would keep me warm.

It would help me hide

on the ice.

fur

I would have small ears on my head.
I would have strong claws on my paws.

Swimming and Eating

I would swim from one piece of ice to another.

I would swim for many hours at a time.

I would have large,
wide paws.

They would help me swim.

I would have bumpy pads on my paws.

The pads would keep me from slipping on the ice.

pad

I would catch and
eat seals.
I would be able to smell
seals through the ice.

Other Behaviors

I would wash myself in the water.

Then I would roll across

the snow.

This would keep my fur clean

and dry.

I would make a hole in the snow.

I would sleep in the hole.

I would have one to three cubs.

They would be able to walk after two months.

Glossary

cub

paw

ice

seal

Index

24